NEERJA

An Indian Woman's Spiritual Odyssey

NAMTA YADAV

Leadstart

ISBN 978-93-5559-031-2

First published in India 2022 by Leadstart Inkstate
A brand of One Point Six Technologies Pvt. Ltd.

123, Building J2, Shram Seva Premises,
Wadala Truck Terminal,
Mumbai 400022, Maharashtra, INDIA
Phone: +91 96999 33000
Email: info@leadstartcorp.com
www.leadstartcorp.com

Disclaimer: This is a work of fiction. All the names, characters, businesses, places, events and incidents in this book are either the product of the author's imagination or used in a fictitious manner. Any resemblance to actual persons, living or dead, or actual events is purely coincidental.

The views expressed in this book are those of the Author and do not pertain to be held by the Publisher.

Editor: Shayoni Mitra
Cover: Komal Kohok
Layouts: Ashwini Rane

Contents

PART ONE   7

A COMPLEX MIND   9
A DETERIORATING BODY   37
A WOUNDED SOUL   67

PART TWO   79

SANGAM   81
SANCTUM SANCTORUM   97
POWER OF KNOWING   101

ABOUT THE AUTHOR

A nature lover and romantic at heart, Namta discovered her affinity for a spiritual life rising to meet the demands of a stressful, modern life. Namta leads a happy, balanced and fulfilled life which she strove to achieve all these years and holds sacred. She aspires to be a spiritual teacher and share her spiritual practice with the rest of the world.

PART ONE

A COMPLEX MIND

Chapter 1

Dusk settled and the clouds parted ways. Clouds never stay in one place for long... if they do, they lose themselves. Amidst the hustle of a small town in India, stood a house surrounded by a few others. Hiding behind this house, a young girl would often converse with some mysterious force! She had visions of *Lord Shiva* when she was younger and secretly performed the *Tandava* when no one was watching. Neerja was one of a kind; the entertainer in a family of four. Their lives were a perfect blend of ups and downs, just like the waves.

Neerja's beauty was noticed right at her birth, she had big almond-shaped eyes, soft pink lips, a sharp nose and long fingers. She was unbelievably quiet, so her existence had to be announced to the neighbours. The seeds of reflection were planted early in her. She had an affinity for nature and cold weather and would fall ill every time the family moved to a hot place. Neerja grew up in the shadow of her virtuous brother Varun, building her own world in her room and in her head. Neither she nor her family knew that this trajectory that she was creating for herself, would lead her to encounters that would jolt them out of their normal lives.

On the surface, her childhood was the easiest part of her life. Beneath the stillness of a lake dwells an entire ecosystem. The glamour of a bureaucratic household, the troupe of servants, a convent school education, and the protective campus life could not stop the winds blowing in her direction. When refused anything, she would throw a tantrum and knew that daddy would come to her rescue. She stayed locked up alone at home one night just because she was not allowed to wear a particular dress to a party. She was wearing a lovely jumpsuit but had seen another girl twirling in her frock downstairs. Her parents pleaded but she did not relent. Stiff branches often break when the winds are strong. Neerja put her foot into the wheel of the bicycle to punish a servant who refused to stop for ice cream on the way back from school; the bone in her tiny ankle cracked. Neerja did not know that when you decide to punish others, you also hurt yourself.

In a middle-class nuclear family, with an ever-expanding circle of relatives, she started struggling to be herself. The constant comparisons with a fairer, taller or brighter cousin left her feeling inadequate. She would often entertain her family post dinner by jumping from one sofa to another like *Hanuman*. They would be delirious with laughter and she would enjoy being the centre of attention before receding to her room where unbeknownst to all, she had been slowly adding another layer of complexity to her mind. Like sedimentary rocks, our minds are shaped by the collection of experiences over the years.

Neerja had already accumulated a few fears of her own along the way. She hated to share anything that she truly loved. She ran with tears rolling down her cheeks when the cameraman took birthday pictures of Neerja's cousin, posing with Neerja's teddy. Neerja had been gifted this teddy by her mother for standing first in her class. Neerja's parents had handed over the teddy to her cousin to please Neerja's uncle. The cousin's birthday was always a grand affair. This incident and the countless others that followed in her childhood broke her heart. She would despise it when her mom would share the design or pattern of Neerja's dresses with her friends who had daughters. Neerja would throw a fit and if she was not obliged, that dress or doll would lose its significance for her. Exclusivity became a norm for her. She either loved someone extremely or they ceased to exist. Nature has shades of light and dark, but Neerja only saw in absolutes.

She shared a deep bond with Varun, they found solace in each other's company during the loud fights at home. They both had their own ways of ignoring the cacophony. Varun burnt the midnight lamp to excel in academics which promised him the golden path to a career in India and a few pats on the back from his Indian parents who believe that children come to this world to fulfil the dreams of their parents. Neerja's vision was blotchy just like her artwork. Neerja's favourite colour was black, her wardrobe always had black. She would protest wildly every time her mom forced her to wear a pink or a yellow dress, she felt that those colours made her look darker.

She was a daredevil; you mess with her brother and she would pick knitting needles to pull out your eyeballs. She would jump on a stubborn horse, be the first one to go parasailing, stand under a chilling waterfall and face competitions on stage fearlessly. It is indeed heart-wrenching to see that strength disappear before your eyes... She first let her fears get the better of her when she tampered with her reports sitting on the bathroom floor in the school. She scratched the grades in her report card with a blade and put higher grades following a friend's advice. She was scared of disappointing her parents and had earned her relief for a few days. The family found out and took their first step on an endless journey of fixing her mistakes.

Neerja had many bright days in her childhood. She relished the special meals her mom cooked for the family. They all ate together and prayed together and so she believed that they would stay together forever. Neerja had an aptitude for languages and started reading the Reader's Digest. She was not exposed to great books as a child but she developed a love for reading. This was the beginning of a lifelong friendship. She excelled at English in school and her essays became exemplary. Math, science and logic flew out of the window. Neerja could never reason out what was good or bad for her. She survived every time she listened to her *inner voice* and hit rock bottom every time she acted on impulse, and she often acted impulsively. Sea beds are pristine and quiet places where pearls of wisdom reside...

Chapter 2

Neerja turned rebellious as a teenager. She would often defy her parents and do what was forbidden. She was naïve and was always misled by her peers. She went to school to be with friends and would chat incessantly with them even while the lessons were being taught. What drove others did not inspire her; marks and grades were never her incentives. She wanted to create moments and her life had plenty of them, both good and bad. She sat on the culvert outside her home one afternoon and refused to eat when the family brought an older cousin home who had long passed the marriageable age as per Indian standards. While her parents were busy grooming this bride to be, Neerja kept feeling the pangs of neglect.

As a reaction to the pain, her mind started building coping mechanisms. She lashed out at her cousins with arrogance, laughing at their lack of money, beauty or sophistication. Since her dad was successful, she used her false sense of superiority to cover the pain that was slowly brewing within her. This was one of the darkest areas that she would have to revisit from her childhood. Every girl secretly believes that she is her dad's princess and when this belief breaks, some develop *Daddy issues*. Many girls seek older partners who would cajole them like a daughter. Even today, in India the birth of a girl child is rarely celebrated, girls are brought up like burdens to be passed on. They are taught to pray for a provider. Life was waiting to surprise Neerja. *The turns in the road often lead to milestones.*

Neerja would dress like a teacher and her dolls and teddies would be her students. She would drape a saree with her mom's *dupatta* and carry a purse and a pile of papers. This became a role that defined her identity for years. Neerja would always return home with flowers and cards after Teachers' Day in appreciation of her work. She yearned for meaning in her work as a teacher and crumpled under the weight of documents. Dolphins love to swim freely; they detest trainers who insist that they jump through the same loops every day.

As adolescents, we need to be taught that we can cultivate love. Neerja did not have a school counsellor growing up. She started believing that the love that had escaped her home was to be found outside. Her parents were caught in broils caused by the constant interference of relatives, a reality that most children growing up in Indian families have to face. Most Indian marriages that begin with the tying up of two families turn into a vendetta. Compared to all this, the outside world had hues; it had fragrances and music, it had magic and a dream that Neerja would chase for the rest of her life. '*The prince and princess meet and fall in love and live happily ever after*' tale has broken many young hearts. Neerja was also in for this scam. Mirages give hope to travellers, but they also delude them.

Neerja was now riding on two delusional horses. She believed that she had to accomplish something extraordinary in order to stand out in the family. She was already battling fat and a body shape that was far from perfect, the beauty of her face could not protect her from the mean comments about her oddly growing trunk and hips. Her cousins compared her to an ostrich. Her mom preferred short hair for her as that was considered modern, adding to Neerja's tomboyish looks.

Lured by a friend, Neerja quit the convent school and went to study in a local school. This was her first co-educational experience; she had convinced her parents on the pretext that she wanted to prepare for medicine and later on try for the prestigious Indian Administrative Services. She had sold them the classic dream that all Indian parents fall for. Soon she lost her grasp over the three sciences and Math became challenging for her. She took refuge in her second delusion. Though she still had conversations with *Shiva*, she waited for a prince to come as her saviour. Her favourite drug now was love; rather her love for love. She knew she loved roses when she got her first from a boy. Thus began the saga – she would bunk school to be with him, write love letters to him with her blood and steal money from the altar to eat in the canteen with friends. She would get beaten by her father when she got caught, but she would never relent. Neerja detested control. Neerja's mother had discovered letters under her sheet, addressed to God asking him to make her mom disappear because she would put sanctions on her. She always felt that her mom favoured her brother though her brother protected his little sister like an angel.

Though Neerja's mom did not keep good health, she was a committed mother who wanted her kids to be perfect in every way. She wanted them to have good features, complexion, teeth, height, scores and health. She took them to the dentist forcing him to put braces on their teeth, gave them carrot juice for that extra inch of height, fasted for them every Tuesday and fed them *laddoos* soaked with *ghee*. Once while her mom had to be rushed to the hospital, the family servant who had raised them as kids started misbehaving. He tried to touch Neerja's back in a perverse manner pretending to clean the back of her chair, Neerja just kept staring into her notebook and never spoke about it. Another servant asked her to come to his room in the servants' quarters when the family was away, and Neerja did report this incident. Her uncle came and beat up the servant with a thick wooden stick.

This clashed with her breakdown due to the pressure that built up before her exams. She was a great procrastinator and was always unprepared. Later in life, Neerja accepted that she could never be forced to do anything. After years of outbursts due to panic, anxiety and stress, she spoke up, *"I can do no more."* She took short chat breaks every half hour. This goldfish was trying to scale a mountain in the final years of school. She barely managed to escape being suspended from school when she tried to miss the Physics exam by making several cuts on her palm with a sharp blade and by lying to her family that her lamp's bulb had exploded on her hand due to overheating at night.

Chapter 3

Neerja was a great storyteller; she would often narrate stories to her mom that she read in books. She was also cooking up some gory stories inside her head. She would knit a yarn like a spider's web and get caught in it. Neerja tried to choke herself with a *dupatta* and cut her wrists and throat. The influence of Bollywood was strong. She slept that night weeping and saying goodbyes to her family in her mind and feeling good that she would be valued and remembered with love. The next morning, she found that she was still alive. The blood had clotted and she had glaring cuts on her wrists and neck. She quickly wore a long full-sleeved cardigan and wrapped a muffler around her neck before her mom came with the milk. Her mom got suspicious and tried to remove the muffler. That evening her dad made her sit on his lap and wept while sipping his whiskey to dull the pain and perhaps the embarrassment.

Varun peeked from his room. He was fighting his own battles; he was preparing to get into the Police Academy because his dad had threatened that he would not pay the fees for an Engineering college if he did not get admission on merit. He did not realise that his father did not mean those words. Their father always got them admitted to the best school in every town. He wanted to be a friend to his children. He would watch cricket excitedly with Varun and woke up every morning before sunrise to take Neerja for a run so that she could grow taller than her mom. Teenage is a very sensitive age and children often misunderstand the intentions of their parents, they are on an emotional roller-coaster. Varun was smart, sincere, simple and brilliant, he should have pursued a career that suited his intellect. Neerja would always put the blame on this innocent soul, every time she fell down as a baby or goofed up as a teenager; she had no qualms about it. She felt passing the blame onto someone would make her problems disappear magically, but they always came back to haunt her later. In the future, she had to spell out loud that she was not the object but the subject in her life.

She enjoyed time with her mother during the last leg of her grade twelve after her brother left for the Police Academy and her father was transferred to the North East. She started to diet and lost a considerable amount of weight. She got unwavering support from her mom who was always willing to keep her happy. Neerja was once again selling dreams. She had set high targets like everyone around her. Her friends were studying for hours to make their middle-class families proud. She was yet to discover the only secret to success -*do what you love, success will follow*. She got the taste of that success after a long time in life when she finally announced, "*I love Literature and I will pursue it.*" As a child, one of her uncles saw great potential in her, he felt that she knew what she wanted to be; she had told him that she would be a teacher someday, and when he asked what would she do after that, she had said that she would be the Principal, on being pestered further, she responded, "*I would be old after that.*"

This clarity in a child's mind is often lost growing up. Her mind started to plot again as the fear of disappointing her mom swelled up. She wished her mom a happy birthday and planted several kisses on her cheeks before leaving for school on the scooter which her parents had gifted her. With just seventy-four rupees in her pocket, she headed to the bus station instead of going to school. She was desperate to save her family from the shame her failure would bring. She spoke softly to the ticket agent through the tiny window and bought a ticket for the bus that was leaving for Lonavala. As the bus slowly moved out of the city and entered the countryside, Neerja started to feel hungry. She turned around and saw a mom feeding her child. Her mom had packed lunch for her but her bag was lying in the scooter that was locked and parked at the bus station. She had broken her mom's trust. The bus reached Lonavala in the evening; once more the divine came to her rescue.

She heard temple bells and walked across the road. She spent several hours sitting on the temple floor wondering what to do, *her inner voice urged her to return home.* In the meanwhile, at home her mom was devastated; the entire campus knew that Neerja had run away from home; the fear for her daughter's life and safety and the gossips and speculations of the neighbours and relatives made her mom anxious; she kept chanting the *Hanuman Chalisa* so that her daughter may return. The police and All India Radio were informed. Her dad flew home immediately shelling out a huge sum of money for the air tickets. Neerja returned home safely the next day with the help of a very kind newly-wed couple whom she approached at the bus station. They were shocked at her thoughtlessness. They paid for her return ticket and put her on a bus.

She first discovered the joy of moving to a new place when she left home to be in a hostel during college. It erased the past from her mind. This became her magic formula for life – out of sight was out of mind. Anytime her cup was brimming with chaos, pain or boredom, it was a signal to move on. She was often requested to stay on by seniors at workplaces, however for Neerja once the mind drifted, the physical shift became necessary. She was heartbroken when she left school. She had broken up with her boyfriend whom she had believed she was in love with. She felt as if she was underwater.

She had a string of one-sided relationships that never manifested into anything real. She kept longing for true love, the kind she had read about in literary classics. She pursued a degree in English Literature from a college situated in a hill station in India where her passion for Literature and her connection with nature intertwined. She would spend days staring at the pine trees outside her window while reflecting on a piece of poetry. She was in her element. She was declared the best user of the library for three consecutive years. She flourished while away from home which was a relief both for her parents and her. *She was finally beginning to carve her individuality.*

Chapter 4

Neerja spent the first year in college attending lectures and pouring over literary classics. She was intrigued by the variety of characters in *The Canterbury Tales* and the humaneness of the *Dickensian* characters. While most literary scholars worship Shakespeare, Neerja proudly declared that she admired Thomas Hardy. She was the *scholar gypsy* in college, that Mathew Arnold described in his poem. Neerja, for the first time, found her mind interestingly engaged in something that did not tire or stress her out. She excelled and was finding her ground.

The warmth of her character was first experienced by her roommate who found Neerja jumping with joy to receive someone into her room Though the betrayal of her friends in school had scarred her and she thought that she had to be guarded, Neerja was soft on the inside. She had convinced herself that opening up to others caused pain and she could avoid being hurt by being closed. But she attracted people naturally, wherever she went.

The next year was different. Neerja was the topper in the first year. Seniors and classmates reached out to her for help and friendship. This was the phase when she discovered her hippie, free-spirited self. She would save her pocket money to make calls to her parents, and to buy books and audio cassettes of rock music. Her Sony Walkman, a Paulo Coelho book and her hippie bag were her constant companions.

She spent hours observing people from the window of the famous Marley Café. Most students spend their college days playing the guitar, listening to music while sipping coffee and building dreams in such cafes. Neerja knew this was what her soul had always longed for. *Her solitude gave her time for introspection.*

She was surrounded by people who shared her interests. They loved *Pink Floyd* and *The Fountainhead*. They were the romantic idealists who believed in love, laughter and lyrics. They relished poetry and worshipped Rumi. Nights were spent in candlelight eating Wai-Wai and preparing for exams. While Neerja was pursuing her favourite subject in college, Varun was completing his training at the Police Academy. He would be an officer soon and his parents were waiting to celebrate their moment of pride. Varun had been diagnosed with a minor heart condition at a young age and was advised to avoid any strenuous physical activity. This boy was now completing one of the toughest physical training programmes to become an officer. Most sons in India carry the burden of their fathers' dreams on their shoulders, few fathers fathom that they may have to carry these young men on their shoulders due to the unwarranted pressures put on them.

Neerja was not oblivious to Varun's plight. He was seething under the hurt of being abandoned, he had expected his family to help him switch his career paths and encourage him to pursue engineering, his preferred subject. Instead, he just kept living the dreams of his parents. She did not know that someday, like Varun, her life would also not be her own until she fought to claim it back. Neerja enjoyed every genre of writing in college; she took a fantastic flip teaching class on *The Tempest* for her peers. They all were in awe and prophesied that Neerja would make a great teacher. Neerja did not get carried away by these praises, she would sit under a tree star-gazing, reading Huxley, while Elton John's *Sacrifice* filled the cool evening breeze on the hilltop. She would light candles at Mother Mary's grotto. She confided in saints more than she did in people.

Like most convent educated girls in the early nineties, she envisioned her life as a nun. Those godly women dressed immaculately in white robes with a rosary around their necks and gospel on their tongues showed that life could be lived differently, your path could be that of devotion. Neerja admired a senior in college, she wept secretly the day that senior graduated. She had learnt to suffer quietly and to put on a tough exterior. She did not realise that our fears turn into demons if we hide them in a closet. Years later when she reconnected with herself, she pulled them all out one by one and faced them. The last year in college was eventful, it was paving the way for what was to come. Neerja came to her parents for the summer break and spent most of her time reading books. She would refuse to attend parties or go on shopping trips with her mom. She was revelling in her newfound Bohemian lifestyle. One evening, her dad insisted that she accompany them to a family friend's house for dinner.

Neerja sat in the drawing-room chatting with the hosts when suddenly an unkempt, tall boy with sharp eyes walked in and sat next to them. The lady of the house introduced him as their son Tejas who was studying at an engineering college. During dinner, his sister invited Neerja to join Tejas and her in the television room. Tejas directed a few questions at Neerja who soon discovered that they had the same taste in books and music. Tejas shared his email address with Neerja. This was the age when the internet was booming and every nook and corner had cyber cafes filled with young adults who were hooked to Hotmail and the world wide web.

When Neerja got back to college she spoke about her new friend to all her buddies. She was unaware of the power of patterns and how the mind can control an individual unless the individual learns to control it. She let her guard down. Soon Neerja began to get tangled in her thoughts and started creating a false narrative.

Chapter 5

One spark was enough to reignite the desire for love in her. Neerja walked into a cyber cafe and typed her first mail to Tejas. She got an instant reply. They began writing to each other and their conversations stimulated her intellectually. She felt she had finally met her *Howard Roark* and their frequencies matched. Neerja's favourite lecturer in college was an unconventional, unmarried woman, she wore khadi and had great knowledge. Neerja admired her and the mentor also saw great potential in Neerja. Neerja was surprised when she gave Neerja, *The Idiot* by Dostoevsky as a parting gift at her graduation with the inscription – *"In recognition of the person you are."* The lecturer knew what Neerja would only realise later. She passed through the corridors of knowledge with her batchmates in college. They all knew and saw in Neerja what she herself was blind to. *They referred to Neerja as a hero. She did not need to find one.*

Neerja was a girl with great integrity. She walked into the principal's office to inform her that all of them were responsible for sneaking in alcohol at the graduation party and those caught should not be the only ones to get reprimanded. She wanted to take responsibility and wanted the whole grade to be held accountable. Her Principal dismissed her from her office but could not ignore the truth in her words. All her life Neerja walked into the offices of her bosses to speak her mind. She never approached anyone for favours but would not keep quiet if someone was wronged. This courage to own her truth was what stood by her in the endless battles she fought, especially later in life. The bruises in her heart shone like hidden medals.

Neerja and Varun were again together at home after a long time. Neerja had graduated from college and Varun had passed out from the Police Academy. They had all returned from his graduation, he was now a commissioned police officer. Neerja was unaware that sometimes the universe gives you time to collect fond memories. She was still the untamed brat like *Catherine* in *Wuthering Heights*. She would revolt in anger if she was told to mend her ways. Varun slapped her one morning for sitting with her legs up on the table while the male servants were serving them breakfast, she protested and demanded that she be allowed to leave the next day for her new job. Neerja was joining a call centre in Mumbai.

Neerja was on a self-destructive path, she was always wondering when the next email from Tejas would arrive. He would respond after weeks and the replies were usually just one-liners. Neerja was trapped in her illusion. She was betraying her love for Literature just to be on her feet. She was also upset with her dad who was now invested in getting another cousin married. Three years in college had given her a taste of independence; she had lost faith in the ability of her parents to either advise or support Varun and her.

Varun had been unwilling to join his family for the lunch post the graduation day parade at the Police Academy. He had braved all odds and won gold medals for academic excellence during the training. Despite all these achievements, he was heartbroken. Often unconsciously, Indian parents encourage their children to compete from an early age. Competition amongst cousins in large families is common. Varun had felt that by joining a career that demanded physical toughness he would snub all the relatives who felt that he would not make it through the training. He believed that he had to make these sacrifices to restore the dignity of his mother, who always shared her woes with her children as a victim of the ill-treatment she received from the members of his father's family in the initial years of their marriage. She had now earned her place and respect in the family through her resilience over the years and had passed on the same lesson to her children: endurance. They had internalised this belief, that they must endure any adversity to maintain the respect of their family in society and amongst relatives.

He stood on the balcony to bid goodbye to Neerja, his little sister. Neerja left in anger not knowing that the skies were quickly changing colours and their darkest hours were now galloping towards them. The bright lights at the multinational company deluded her, she spent all her earnings on cigarettes and outings with colleagues. Luckily, Neerja was blessed with two angels in disguise as her roommates in her paying guest accommodation who did not allow her to accept an invitation to a rave party where her colleagues were planning to try drugs. *God never abandons us. He takes care of us in his own ways.*

Neerja kept in touch with Tejas via email and one day he wrote to her that he was coming to Mumbai to meet her. Neerja and her roommate hired a cab and left for the railway station. Neerja wore a lemon-yellow tank top, black pyjamas and slung across her shoulder was her favourite hippie bag with a few cigarettes in it. The matte brown lipstick and the dark kajal with her hair tightly clasped at the back allowed her luscious lips, almond-shaped eyes and chiselled nose to be highlighted. Tejas looked nervous as he stepped down a crossover bridge to get to the platform where Neerja was standing. He looked a bit weathered and was avoiding eye contact. He slowly relaxed as the three of them sat around and chatted in a pub. He left the next day and called Neerja from college. Tejas told her he did not want any emotional involvement; sex, drugs, rock and roll, the counter culture was what he was invested in at college. He had only wanted to hook up.

Varun was leaving for his first mission as a police officer to Telangana and decided to visit Neerja. Neerja's parents joined him and pulled him into accompanying them to meet a few possible alliances for Neerja in Mumbai. Varun warned them before leaving for duty that Neerja was not ready for marriage yet. In the meantime, Neerja kept wishing secretly that Tejas would develop feelings for her someday.

After a couple of months, a strong wind caused the curtain next to Neerja's bedside to drop her favourite coffee mug. Neerja always drank her coffee from it at home, curled up with a book much to the envy of Varun who would teasingly come and sit on her bed next to her. One such moment was captured in a picture that hung in Neerja's bedroom.

Chapter 6

Neerja was intuitive since childhood; she felt very uneasy. Just then she heard the landlady screaming her name and her urgent footsteps on the stairs. She quickly handed over the phone to Neerja. Neerja's mom broke down on the phone and since that day, her words never stopped ringing in Neerja's ears, *"Varun is no more. He took his last breath fighting the Naxalites."* Neerja slid down the stairs with tears rolling down her face.

No one is ever prepared for the death of a loved one. As the saying goes, *"God plucks his prettiest flowers the soonest"*. Varun was only twenty-two years old. Neerja returned home; the house was eerily silent. To her dismay, her parents were sitting in two separate rooms each surrounded by their own relatives. Neerja was torn and awakened to the reality of a divided house once again. Her parents were lifeless and she had to take responsibility. Varun arrived in a coffin that was wrapped in the Indian flag as he had died on duty and was a promising young officer. The body was flown down and was handed over to the family after the postmortem. Relatives began to arrive and the neighbours opened up their hearts and homes. They had seen the glorious days of this family; they remembered a proud father who would not stop praising his children.

Even if you close your fist very tightly, sand and water always find a way to pass through. Neerja opened the coffin and saw the blue face of her brother. The relatives slowly brought the parents close to the body, still holding onto them knowing that they would lose control seeing their young son confined to a box that he was not going to leave. In India, the last rites are performed by the son or a male member of the family however Neerja's dad had raised her as an equal. He asked the pandit to allow Neerja to be the one to conduct the rites for her brother. This offended a few relatives who had already created an unpleasant scene between her parents by tattling.

Tejas's parents came to express their condolences and Neerja's eyes searched for him. But he was missing. Neerja left for the cremation grounds and watched her father light the pyre of his only son; the worst punishment a parent could ever face.... Neerja was now both their son and daughter. She could feel the burden shift onto her shoulders and missed Varun sorely. He was her guardian and now she felt vulnerable and confused. She had a lot of pent-up resentment towards her parents. Once the relatives left, within a few days after Varun's death, she went back to her old ways and began watching movies, going shopping and was even caught smoking in the toilet at home. She told her parents how she had befriended Tejas and wished to get married to him.

Her dad had known the family for a long time and was happy with the prospect, though he knew that Neerja was too immature for marriage. She convinced her dad to give her a chance to meet Tejas and to find out his feelings. She set off for the British Council Library and waited for three hours. When she finally stepped out, she received a call from Tejas saying that he had completely forgotten about their meeting.

Her mother was disheartened as slowly all the families that once dreamt of seeing Neerja as their daughter-in-law, were now backing off from the proposal. They were an unfortunate family that had a young death and were outcast by society that was both wary and sceptical about the well-being of their own sons. The tables had turned, Time was against them and the birds of merriment were migrating. In desperation, Neerja's mother forced Neerja's father to get a matrimonial advertisement published in a newspaper for Neerja.

Neerja had quit her job at the call centre and was working to clear the entrance test for admission to the Master's program at Mumbai University. She was called for an interview by a renowned college but instead of focusing on her preparation, she kept hoping that this accomplishment would win her Tejas's validation, who was now at a famous management institute. Later on in life, Neerja realised the *power of intention* listening to a conversation between her spiritual role model Oprah Winfrey and the legendary Wayne Dyer. Her intention was wrong and the Universe was not going to grant her wish. She had to get affiliated with another college to attend her Master's course at Mumbai University. She hated the humid weather, the dusty libraries and her roommate in the paying guest accommodation.

She bunked lectures regularly as she missed the protective environment of her college in the hills. She had lost that paradise and by now, Tejas had cut off from her completely. Her days were spent reading books on pavements and the nights were spent at discs with her friends. She loved the beach and enjoyed the colours and flavours that life in Mumbai offers. Towards the end of the first year, she joined her parents for the wedding of her cousin. Neerja had turned egotistical, her beauty got the attention of prospective grooms in their community. She would disrespect and scream at her parents who were now enemies in her eyes. She blamed their negligence for Varun's death in front of all the relatives and they were heartbroken. They felt that she needed to be settled by way of marriage. In the heat of the moment, her father went out and made a call to Mayur's family who had shown interest in the matrimonial advertisement in the newspaper. After reading about her in the matrimonial column a few days before the cousin's wedding, Mayur had come to meet Neerja as his prospective bride, at her paying guest accommodation in Mumbai.

Since she was not living with her parents in Pune, but studying in Mumbai, they had arranged for him to visit her to get to know her.

Neerja had a high pony and was dressed in a black salwar suit. Mayur just kept staring at her as she spoke freely. She then sat on the pavement and sipped her favourite local coffee. He was impressed by her ability to adjust to any environment. Mayur who had not married until the age of thirty despite all attempts by his family made up his mind in ten minutes. He excused himself and made a call to his parents stating that he was ready to get married. For Neerja this was sheer fun, she told her friends that she was going to enjoy a good laugh at his cost over a few cups of coffee.

Mayur and his family had not expected this sudden call from Neerja's dad as Neerja's parents had not shown any interest after seeing Mayur. They felt Mayur's looks and the age difference between Neerja and Mayur would make them incompatible.

Neerja's parents were annoyed with Neerja's behaviour at her cousin's wedding and were unhappy with her life in Mumbai. They reacted impulsively to her misbehaviour by going to Varanasi after the cousin's wedding to formalise her alliance with Mayur despite her opposition. Neerja knew she was going to fail her Master's program and saw this as the door that promised escape. Neither her parents nor Neerja knew that their blurred vision was leading her down a rather dark alley; a black hole that would engulf and steal her essence completely.

A DETERIORATING BODY

Neerja packed her belongings to leave her student life behind and step into the next phase of her life. Her father took his princess in his arms in disbelief at the sudden realisation that he would be passing her onto another man. The entire life of most Indian women is divided between two households. One is their father's, where they reside after their birth and the other is their husband's which they are expected to leave only after their death. Any other option is still unfavourable if not unimaginable. The days or months before the engagement and the wedding are just spent preparing the young bride. Neerja was made to join a fitness centre so that she could shed a few pounds. Her diet was controlled and various age-old natural remedies were prescribed for her hair and skin. The bride must glow at the wedding just like the banquet hall.

The irony of the big fat Indian weddings (that are arranged by the families) is that the bride and bridegroom who have met only a couple of times promise each other a lifetime of togetherness before the holy fire. It's like making an investment blindfolded. Neerja was thrilled because of the care and attention that she was receiving at home. The fancy sarees, jewellery and trips to the market and parlour had clouded her reasoning. Mayur arrived at Pune a few days before the wedding and they both were delighted to spend time with each other. They had already experienced the joy of holding hands, cosy hugs and had felt each other's bodies on a short trip that Mayur had made to Mumbai earlier. This was right after the alliance was formalised, by the popular *roka* ceremony. Indian teenagers are not encouraged to explore their sexuality and are not provided sex education at home or school, these topics are hushed and when they get the permit to do so in the form of a marriage certificate their hormones explode. Everything seems rosy and chemical reactions are often mistaken for true love.

Neerja and Mayur were inseparable for those few days. He would land up at her door early in the morning and would leave at night. It was New Year's Eve and they decided to go to a disc. Neerja wore a red cardigan and a pair of dark blue jeans. She enjoyed drinking and danced freely. When she was at a party, only fun ruled. Mayur felt the first pang of insecurity seeing her sipping down the last drop of vodka from her glass. He noticed that Neerja had a spirit that could not be contained. He wanted them to leave for dinner. They parked their car outside an Indian *dhaba* and decided to eat in the car. Neerja relished non-vegetarian food and was engrossed in her own world when she suddenly glanced at Mayur who was fuming. There were men on motorbikes who had surrounded their car and were staring at Neerja. Neerja ignored them and kept eating. This made Mayur lose his temper.

He accused Neerja of being self-absorbed and reckless. That night she saw something in his face that seemed like a warning. When they returned home, she bid him goodbye and crept into bed. The next morning, she told her parents that things were not fine. Mayur was not someone Neerja could live with and she found his behaviour stifling. Later that day when Mayur came to pay them a visit, he brought along a bouquet to apologize to Neerja who had refused to see him. He convinced Neerja's mother that he was remorseful and was concerned about Neerja. Neerja had locked herself up in the bathroom and did not listen to her mother. Mayur was resolute and begged for another chance. It is not easy for common people to see through a facade or to identify signs of a psychological disorder. They all relented one by one.

This was the beginning of the torture that Neerja would have to undergo for the next ten years. This is often the plight of many Indian women, who enter into an arranged marriage and do not know the stranger they are sent off to spend the rest of their lives with. Many get married to narcissists, male chauvinists, psychopaths, sociopaths, violent or promiscuous men and perish in such arrangements. The stress of getting married at an early age does not allow the girl to develop her independent thinking and to discover her individuality. They become the shadows of these men who neither love nor value them. Neerja's cries were trapped within bathroom walls for years, trying to understand why she was subjected to this suffering.

Another episode followed soon before the wedding during which Mayur revealed a very different side of his nature. After which, like the classic Indian villain, he used the trump card of respectability to get Neerja's mother to her knees! If Neerja broke the engagement, what would she and her family explain to the guests who had already received the wedding cards and the neighbours, who had seen him leaving their house every night? The marriage was close and Neerja's family got busy with the preparations. Mayur tried forcing Neerja to lose more weight close to the wedding. Neerja was in good shape and could not at the time decipher that these attacks were meant to destroy her sense of self-worth. They experienced a sense of uneasiness and like Mayur's parents, had a feeling that Mayur was not a suitable match for Neerja. Mayur negated the objections of his parents who were shocked when they first saw Neerja. Their faces showed their disapproval but their son silenced them. There was something that they seemed to be hiding. Neerja and her parents were still grieving over Varun's death and did not even try to get to the bottom of this mystery.

Neerja made all heads turn towards her as she walked down the aisle. Dressed in heavy lehengas, laden with jewellery and make-up, most Indian brides sit on the stage like dolls for hours, as guests come and bless the newlyweds. Unfortunately, in many cases, the bridegrooms' families look for ways of extorting money in the form of dowry either before or after the marriage, but all this generally happens behind the scenes. Mayur's family had affirmed right from the beginning that they would not accept anything except Neerja who was now their 'daughter'. This had assured Neerja's parents that she was going to the right family as after Varun's death, Neerja was their only child and would inherit everything they had built.

Chapter 8

A day before the wedding, Neerja's mother was informed by the hotel staff that Mayur's mother was complaining about the arrangements for their stay. When she approached Mayur, he said that the arrangements were fine, but there should have been something for the relatives to see. Mayur's ambiguous statement made Neerja's mother nervous. Neerja was about to put the garland around Mayur's neck when his family pulled him back, a usual prank played at most Indian weddings. She tried again but they pulled him back once more. She made the third attempt and he still moved back. Neerja's parents felt giddy as they were staying spirited despite the death of their young son. They requested that it was a sombre occasion for them and the rituals must be performed with devotion. Mayur finally consented and garlands were exchanged. There were soft murmurs amongst the crowd Most guests wondered what had prompted Neerja and her parents to accept this man. His bloodshot eyes and broad grin were alarming.

The most auspicious part of the wedding began. Mayur remarked jokingly that it was difficult for him to put his arms around Neerja. Neerja did not pay heed to these hurtful comments. She was living her moments. Though she had a western outlook, she was also deeply rooted in traditions. She loved wearing glass bangles and put the vermilion religiously throughout her married life; it was a craving that never left her. Her *mangalsutra* was unique and she had chosen it herself. After the *pheras* around the holy fire and the exchange of vows, the couple sought the blessings of the elders. Dinner was served and Mayur again teased Neerja by pulling away the spoon every time she opened her mouth to receive a morsel from him. He told her that his gaze was focused on Neerja's unmarried cousin during the ceremony.

Neerja did not know that the companion whom she had vowed to spend her life with assuming that he loved her was hiding a childhood complex about his unpleasant looks and short height. Neerja justified her decision in her mind as she believed in the goodness of people more than their looks. She was unaware that she was just a trophy wife with good looks, education and money to caress Mayur's wounded ego before his family and friends. Neerja's in-laws also acted strangely at the wedding. When Neerja walked to the hotel room with Mayur, he had already consumed alcohol and encouraged Neerja to drink as well. Neerja was scared, she could not give herself fully to Mayur that night. She had heard that intercourse would hurt the first time and closed herself tightly. The next day they visited her parents and set off for their pilgrimage to *Vaishno Devi* which was followed by their honeymoon at Goa. All the arrangements for the trips were done by Neerja's father who had also borne the entire expenditure for the trips. Grooms are often showered with gifts in different forms in India. Most Indian parents feel that they need to appease the groom's family so their daughters are treated well in their husband's home. Especially in a society, where the joint-family system still prevails in several areas and most important decisions are taken only by the elders of the family, whether it concerns them or not!

Mayur would flare up over small issues and would sulk for hours during their honeymoon. Every time Neerja wore an attractive piece of clothing, he would insist that they spend their time together inside their hotel room. She urged him to go sightseeing with her but he was unwilling. Mayur avoided spending any money on Neerja and did not allow her to shop. His enjoyment with her was purely physical and he kept her indoors. Neerja had no elder sister or a close friend who could educate her about the physical pleasures. Like most Indian parents, hers had also tried to preserve Neerja's innocence, but this had only left her ignorant about her own needs. She accepted that Mayur's pleasure was hers too and spent several years, remaining detached from her own body. She thought her body was only a means to keep Mayur close and she satisfied herself through that intimacy. But, soon Neerja was tired of being locked up in the house. All the dreams that a new bride sees were fading for her. She contemplated going back to work, but realised that she was already in the family way! Her pregnancy changed the course of her life.

Both the families were elated with the news but for separate reasons. Neerja's mother believed that Varun was returning to them as Neerja's child and her in-laws were hoping that they would be blessed with a grandson this time; they already had two granddaughters from their older son who had refused to try for a boy the third time. They ran to the astrologer who confirmed the birth of a baby boy. Mayur became even more controlling. He asked Neerja to keep her pregnancy a secret from their friends and told her to refrain from accepting invitations to any gatherings. Her face and spirit were slowly dulled and she forgot what it meant to be carefree. Neerja gradually soaked herself in the joy that pregnancy offers. The care shown by strangers, warm smiles at the nursing home, watching your belly bump grow in a mirror and the kicks of the baby are memories that every woman makes during those months and stores in her treasure chest. Neerja was saving each one of them. Their joy knew no bounds when the doctor told them that it was a healthy round-faced baby. Neerja and the doctor then caught Mayur staring at the ultrasound sound screen, he explained that he was trying to look for the tiny toes and fingers. They all smiled at the wonder of a new life. Neerja felt that Mayur was softening as she was carrying their child. We always hold onto hope.

Mayur called from the office after a few days to tell Neerja that he was nominated to go on a professional development course which had always been his dream. It was a six months long course. They had just begun to bond as parents but Neerja did not want to stand in the way of his dreams and she decided to fly down to her parents. They were returning from dinner outside that night and in a rush, Mayur banged his car into the one in front of him. Neerja's head hit the front shield and she clutched her husband's hand tightly, her eyes closed due to the shock. They ran to the washroom on returning home and were relieved that the baby was fine. This was the third time he had been careless enough to get into an accident during her pregnancy. Neerja developed a phobia and felt scared all her life sitting in the front seat of any vehicle. The next morning before she left, Mayur kissed her forehead and divulged that he was in fact trying to figure out the gender of the child that day by staring at the ultrasound screen!

Neerja's in-laws called her every week while Mayur slowly got busy with his course. Her parents were overjoyed to have

Neerja with them. They were now aware of the problems in her marriage. They were troubled by the fact that Neerja had lost her freedom and confidence. She had been confined to a dark cell. Neerja had already suffered from pigmentation in college, her skin slowly started getting darker. She put on weight on her hips and her belly was now covered with stretch marks. Neerja who was always so proud of her beauty had now become careless. Her husband had a jealous and possessive nature and Neerja was abused if she wore make-up, sleeveless tops or skirts. He would keep lying in bed so that they would reach the get-togethers and parties late just to demoralise Neerja. Neerja did not understand that *loving yourself is the greatest gift that you can give to yourself.* The most profound lesson that Neerja learnt after her initiation into spirituality later on in life was that you must love and care for yourself before helping others. The analogy of picking up the crying baby first, shared by *Brahma Kumari* Sister Shivani during one of her talks, explained that just as a mother puts everything aside to tend to her crying baby, a person must drop everything else or forget about others and tend to themselves first when they are hurting. Only a cup that is brimming or overflowing with self-love can be of help to others. This also made her realise that by not pulling down her oxygen mask and wearing it first, Neerja had done a great disservice to herself all those years.

Chapter 9

Neerja was slowly beginning to relax in the comfort of her parents' home. They came close as a family of four again. The baby's movements inside her belly cheered them up. Her father got fresh fruits from the market every day and her mom would prepare nutritious Indian delicacies to ensure that the baby was healthy. Most Indian daughters become closer to their families after their marriage. They respect the sacrifices their parents made and the parents also do their best to secure the married life of their daughters.

It was the day of the Lunar eclipse and following the age-old Indian traditions Neerja's mom had refrained her from cutting, sewing or sleeping during odd hours. Neerja suddenly received a phone call from Mayur that evening. He sounded distressed. He told Neerja that his seniors were trying to harm him and that he had failed in the professional course he was attending. Neerja was upset as this was the dream for which she had agreed to leave him during a period that most couples spend together. Neerja's mother walked into the room and caught her crying. Neerja was rubbing her eyes and this flustered her mother. She asked Neerja to calm down as she feared that this might affect the baby's health. Neerja broke the news to her in-laws who asked her to focus on the baby. They told her that they were busy preparing gifts and were eager to come and see their grandson.

Neerja's delivery date was still a month away. The next

evening Neerja's parents decided to take her out for dinner to celebrate her birthday. She was unprepared for what was to come. Her phone rang and Mayur's friend first wished her and then told her that he was concerned about Mayur. He disclosed that Mayur had been caught stealing exam papers and an official enquiry was being conducted on him. Neerja quickly called Mayur and detected his first big lie. Instead of feeling guilty about lying to her, he started screaming at her. He accused her of being inconsiderate. Neerja succumbed to his temper and allegations and went out with her parents that evening. They had arranged for a cake and some flowers to make this day special for their daughter. Unfortunately, the whole evening was spent discussing Mayur's misdoings. That night Neerja woke up in a pool of water. Her mom sprang up and woke up Neerja's dad. Neerja's waterbag had burst!

Ordeals are deal breakers in most relationships. They expose the façade. The doctor was negligent and took several hours to attend to Neerja. The baby had the umbilical cord wound around its neck and its heartbeat started dropping. Neerja was rushed to the operation theatre and she faintly heard the doctor asking for forceps and then announcing the birth of a baby girl. Her daughter's first cry and her body covered in blood nauseated Neerja who just slipped into unconsciousness. She woke up several hours later, her body was shivering and her stitches hurt. The nurse held Neerja's daughter close to her. She was wearing the yellow baby suit that her parents had purchased with her for the baby. Neerja disliked the baby the first time she saw her for some unknown reason. She was fair and her nose resembled Mayur's. Neerja was overpowered by a feeling of fear lying in her bed in the ICU, she was dreading the reactions of everyone outside.

The families had been expecting a grandson.

Neerja had hoped to win their hearts by giving them a boy. *The Universe was trying to jolt her out of the lie that she had been living for a year now.* Neerja's father informed Mayur and his family about the birth of the baby girl. Mayur was in disbelief, he felt that the news was false. Neerja's in-laws reacted coldly and showed no interest in coming down to see the child. Mayur unwillingly arrived the next day and seemed distant. The baby's right eye did not open at birth for some reason. That night, for the first time, Neerja and Mayur took care of their daughter together in the hospital room. Neerja had never seen such a tiny baby and was struggling to nurse her.

The caesarean left her feeling weak and drowsy. Mayur expressed his family's displeasure with the choice of the nursing home. He said that this decision had resulted in the baby's right eye being affected. They got into a heated argument and in a fit of anger Mayur hit Neerja with the blanket on her stitches. When the nurse came to check on her, she noticed that Neerja's blood pressure was low. The next morning the baby was very sick and had developed a stomach infection. She was a premature baby and was sent to the incubator. Neerja's parents came to visit them that evening and brought some soup for her. Although they asked Mayur to serve it to Neerja, they noticed that Mayur was busy with his mobile while the soup was turning cold. Mayur's mask had fallen, he was brazen-faced and unabashed!

After three days the baby paid a visit to her parents with the nurse. Neerja held her in her arms and caught the baby looking at her with her small eyes, she had a drip in her nose. At that moment the baby's smell and innocence moved

Neerja as nothing had done before. Neerja experienced an emotion that was completely foreign to her. She eagerly waited to take her cherub home. Neerja immersed herself in motherhood and they were all engrossed in taking care of the baby together. Neerja just kept holding on to these scattered moments of hope.

A few months had passed by, and Neerja felt that since her in-laws had not seen her baby, it was her duty to visit them. She left with Mayur and the baby to be with them. Neerja did not know that all her illusions were going to shatter and her world would crumble like a stack of cards. Mayur's family sent Neerja and her baby to a room that was at the far end of the house. Her mother-in-law asked Neerja to dry the baby's clothes inside and not to step out at all. Neerja was confused, she was aware that they had longed for a grandson but did not imagine that the stigma attached to the birth of a girl child could be so far-reaching. They did not want anyone to know that they were blessed with their third granddaughter. It was ironic as her in-laws worshipped the *Devis* and fasted for nine days during the *Navratris* but were embarrassed at the birth of a girl child.

Chapter 10

Neerja's daughter Diya was diagnosed with congenital Ptosis in the right eye, a drooping eyelid in layman's language. Neerja was giving a massage to Diya one day when her mother-in-law walked into the room. She instructed Neerja that if the neighbours came to see the baby, Neerja must tell them that she had injured the baby's right eye with her elbow, hence it was not opening perfectly. When Neerja tried to confront her mother-in-law, she burst out in anger. Neerja was left speechless as she heard words come out of her mother in-laws' mouth that were as sharp as arrows.

They were disappointed that Neerja had not brought any dowry and accused her family for the birth of the girl child! What hurt Neerja most was that they had not expressed any such demands before the wedding. Their true intentions surfaced now. Neerja had heard about Indian brides being burnt for dowry or ridiculed for the birth of a girl child but she never expected that something like this would happen to her. She believed that this happened to helpless women. She had grown with privileges and her mind was trying to negate this experience. She was in denial.

The next day Neerja's mother called and both the families got into a huge fight on the phone. All the ceremonies, sweet talks and promises lost their significance. The hollowness and the superficiality of customs shook Neerja. This alliance meant a lot to her family, she knew that her parents were not ready for another blow. Losing a young son and a married daughter's return to her father's home are considered the worst tragedies in Indian society, it is considered a taboo in most communities. Neerja was now the mother of a girl child and at the mercy of her husband. She left her in-laws' home with Mayur after a few weeks. Mayur would spend all his time in the office and Neerja was confined to the house.

Her outer beauty had dwindled. She was a nursing mother and her body was going through hormonal changes. Neerja slipped into depression and started stress eating. Mayur had turned violent and even threatened to throw acid on her during one of the fights. Neerja would also lash out in frustration then she would put Diya in a pram and go out to get some fresh air. She was ashamed that she had fallen so low. Varun's words echoed in her ears. He often warned Neerja that giving the steering wheel of her life in someone else's hands would push her into an abyss someday. She decided to teach Mayur and his family a lesson for treating a girl child unfairly. Neerja was suffering from a chronic urinary infection and left for her parents' home for treatment. She wanted Mayur to take care of their daughter but to her dismay when she called Mayur that evening to check on Diya, Mayur revealed that Diya had been sent to live with his parents and they had taken a unanimous decision that they did not want Neerja to be a part of their famila. She must never return.

Neerja dropped the phone and ran to her parents to break the news; the next morning, she was on the train to Varanasi. Mayur's parents were pleased to see Neerja at their doorstep in such a frenzied state. She begged them to let her in and to take Diya with her. She was forced to return. Neerja spent a month wailing for her daughter, she would moan and wake up her parents at night. Her daughter was the second person she truly loved after Varun. She did not want to lose her as well. Her parents then reached out and offered a blank cheque to Mayur, they wanted their daughter to have her child back, it was unbearable for them to see Neerja suffer so much. Neerja decided that she would not give up, this was a mother's battle and Neerja donned her armour and shield, like *Joan of Arc;* she came back empty-handed several times. Neerja gathered her inner strength and refused to leave her in-laws' doorstep without her daughter, she was manhandled and a cloth was stuffed in her mouth so that her groans could not be heard but she did not relent. Finally, her in-laws got scared that their neighbours might inform the police as some of them were beginning to get suspicious that something was amiss.

The family never wanted to raise Diya, they just wanted to see Neerja bend and break before their eyes and to extort money from her parents. They eventually returned the child and Neerja went back to Mayur. She did not want Diya to be deprived of the love of both her parents. Neerja believed that by sacrificing herself she could save Diya and her parents from the pain and hurt that is caused by a broken home or a failed relationship. From her childhood, Neerja had always been scared of failing and disappointing her loved ones. Now also, she felt that she must try till the very end.

Neerja's love for Diya became her weakness. Mayur now had the control in his hands. She was isolated and put in a separate room. He would not speak to her and neither was she allowed to call her parents. Mayur would only visit her room for his physical gratification; he would tie her hands to the bed, play pornographic films in the background and would fulfil his fantasies. Neerja had been reduced to a toy. Mental abuse can do more damage to a person than physical abuse, as the victim suffers quietly and the scars are invisible.

Neerja's parents had gifted Mayur a car to appease him after Diya's birth. Since Neerja already knew how to drive, she decided to drive her daughter to a playschool every day. On one such day, the head of the school stopped her to speak to her. A teacher at the playschool was leaving and they were looking for a replacement. She offered the position to Neerja. Neerja was pleasantly surprised. She decided to take up the offer to gain her financial independence. It would also be a way of keeping herself occupied in that empty home and relationship of hers. Needless to say, it would also be a way of being around Diya all the time.

Nonetheless, Mayur threw a tantrum when he learnt that Neerja had taken up a job. He came down heavily on her, and once again Neerja acted impulsively. One night when Mayur visited her room for his gratification she foolishly convinced him to get physical with her without any protection. She believed that if they had another child together their issues would be resolved. She did not understand that you do not bring children into this world to fix your problems but you only sign up to be parents when you are ready to provide them with a healthy environment. Mayur refused to support her through this pregnancy, he wanted them to wait and plan for a son.

In India, a lot of self-proclaimed medicine men advertise herbal pills that ensure the birth of a son. There is still a mafia of few chemists, ultrasonologists and doctors in small parts of India that is involved in female infanticides. These stories were not unfamiliar to Neerja, but nobody expects the worst can happen to them. *Neerja was making unconscious choices. Her inner voice had become meek due to this outer conundrum.* Her husband's abuse was now directed towards the unborn child. He kicked her womb on a certain occasion and told her that this child was unwanted. Mayur was dreading the birth of another girl as that would offend his parents.

Neerja's parents were also hurt by her decision to be pregnant again. She gave in to the pressure created on her by Mayur and went to a doctor whom Mayur knew personally for an ultrasound scan to find out the gender of the foetus. They discovered that once again it was a female foetus and Neerja was moved to the operation theatre once more in her life. Unfortunately, this time it was not to bring new life into the world but to end it. She kept hoping that her husband would change his mind and pull her out of the operation theatre. He would fight for their child and love would triumph over fear. She lost and her womb was empty.

This incident broke Neerja. She knew this crack in their relationship would never heal. She experienced what so many women in India do, her background, education, ideals, beauty or pleas could not save her from facing reality and confronting her own guilt. Later in life, Diya became a staunch feminist. She often wondered why women have to pay such a heavy price for love in this world. She had witnessed her mom's life closely and realised that society allows this oppression of women; they are raped openly on streets and bashed furtively behind closed doors.

Chapter 11

Neerja lost faith in life, she clung to Diya and saw herself only as a mother now. Every other relationship had betrayed and hurt her. She observed how society put pressure on men as well, they were raised to be dominant. Her father had once commanded Mayur to act like a man and not give in to Neerja's whims; the male gynaecologist they had visited a few weeks after their wedding because Neerja was still intimidated and they were unable to consummate their marriage, had given Mayur the same advice, *"Push forcefully. Be a man."* Winning the affection and trust of a woman is never considered important just possessing her is. Both boys and girls should be taught about consent growing up.

Neerja wanted to give her daughter the finest education. She decided it was time to make some small changes in her life. She started living with her parents and working in an eminent school and her daughter was admitted there. Neerja who had lost a few years in this grind called 'life' and in the efforts to save her marriage agreed to start as a fresher. Despite her degree in Literature, she joined as a primary teacher. There are no stepping stones in life that cannot be turned into bigger opportunities. Teaching a primary grade required all the skills that Neerja never cared to cultivate. She had to learn art and craft and above all patience. Neerja's parents were now dedicated to supporting their daughter in every way possible. Her dad made it his mission to help

Neerja complete her education and help her find a foothold. Financial independence always empowers a woman.

Neerja spent hours perfecting her charts, teachers' diaries and handwriting on a whiteboard. Diya watched her closely, she showed signs of intelligence early on and was a high achiever. Neerja focused on her child's overall growth and never put any pressure on her to excel. This was the mantra that helped Diya to excel. Diya always exclaimed, *"Mom, unlike other parents you always allow me to learn without worrying about grades. This is the reason I have developed an interest in academics. I simply enjoy it!"*

After three years of hard work, Neerja's work started to win recognition. *The Universe always has a plan. There is always a key to a locked door.* Life can never be meaningless, sometimes we find that meaning by walking through fire and sometimes by diving deep into the ocean. This quote resonates with us all, *"When God is not walking beside you, he is carrying you in His arms."* Neerja started writing creative pieces and poetry, she sounded great on a mic. She was the natural choice for a compere for any event.

The family planned to get Diya's right eye operated on by the best doctor in the country. They wanted to save the child from developing a complex while growing up. The decision was a bit rushed as the doctor promised to rectify the problem and they trusted him blindly. Life had more challenges in store for Neerja. Sometimes she would regret the years she lost and the pain she had to endure, during such weak moments Diya would remind her how these lessons had transformed Neerja into an empathetic person. The brat who used to bully her brother was now softening through tears and tribulations.

Neerja and Mayur again got into an ugly fight that night at the hospital. She was a strong woman in the outside world but always allowed herself to be victimised by men. She felt empty without a relationship and wanted to piggyback on a man. Diya's bandages came off after a few days. When the stitches came off, they realised that the results were not positive. This was a strange stroke of misfortune; the doctor was assisted by his interns who operated under the doctor's supervision, and instead of the problem in the right eye being corrected, Diya's left eye was also left spoilt. This was a famous hospital and a very reputed doctor; nothing seemed to prevent the catastrophes lined up for Neerja and Diya.

Mayur was getting transferred to a different city. Neerja made an impulsive move, she gave up her job, left her parents' home once again and went with him. Since the operation was unsuccessful, she felt that she had failed. She convinced herself that she needed to keep trying unselfishly to give Diya a home like other children and was willing to give up her job to work on her marriage yet again. Girls in India are raised to believe that the onus of making the marriage work, lies on them and they must sacrifice themselves for the happiness of others. Neerja was making a mistake but she believed that she was making the right decision. She was conditioned to believe that keeping things together is right and breaking a relationship though easy, was wrong. After all, no one in her family had gone through a divorce.

They missed the train and spent the night at a cheap motel and boarded a Volvo the next day. Diya was unhappy with the decision; she loved her old school and her grandparents' home. This was the worst decision Neerja ever took for her daughter. Neerja was now in her thirties, she felt feverish after a few days and noticed a rash on her belly. They went to the local doctor who diagnosed that Neerja had Chickenpox and cautioned them about the complications of contracting it at her age.

Neerja was subjected to more pain. She was locked up in a room and was forced to eat whatever was available. The blisters slowly covered her entire face and body. She was unable to swallow spicy food and if she complained she would get beaten. Mayur twisted her fingers one day, her wedding ring caused the blister between her fingers to burst and the sore refused to dry for weeks. Diya tried to come to Neerja's rescue but was pushed and her head hit the bed, the back of her head started to bleed. Neerja had dragged her daughter into this hell, and her obstinacy had begun to harm her daughter's mental and physical well-being. Diya had matured before her age; her childhood was lost. Young minds are very impressionable. Neerja was trying to achieve the impossible. She was trying to change someone else.

She kept the *Karva Chauth* fast (a day-long fast that Indian women keep, to pray for the long lives of their husbands) despite her medications. The women break their fasts upon seeing the moon and by drinking water and receiving a morsel of sweet or food from the hands of their husbands. Her head was bursting with pain but she performed her puja. Mayur did not participate and just kept a bar of chocolate lying in the house as a sweet. During the first year, he had also fasted with her. After the conflict between the two families, things never got normal. Need-based relationships are the worst, as long as you fulfil each other's needs the drive is smooth, but the moment those needs are not met or new ones arise the marriage goes off the track. The partners live under the same roof but in separate and individual worlds.

Chapter 12

Neerja slowly recovered. Diya was admitted to a local school and Neerja would prepare her tiffin and drop her at the bus stop every morning. During this period Neerja cooked meals, arranged parties and built a relationship with Mayur's older brother and his wife. She had already bonded with the nieces after her marriage and was keen that her daughter mingled with her cousins. She celebrated her daughter's birthday with pomp and organised several games for children. Her talent and creativity slowly gained everyone's admiration. The theme-based parties she would arrange became the talk of the town.

Unfortunately, at home, Neerja would still succumb to physical violence. She would find her clothes in empty cartons thrown outside the house or rolled up in Mayur's shoes. Her eye pencils and jewellery lay broken in his cupboard. Diya would witness her mother being thrown off a chair and kicked with heavy shoes. Mayur was turning vicious and insulting; he would praise other women before Neerja, boycott any social event where she was playing the role of the compere or the organiser and denied her any affection or closeness. This was also the stage in her life when Neerja learned to pleasure herself; she experienced several emotions, she felt embarrassed because she had been ignorant for so long, guilty because she realised that she never felt fulfilled with Mayur and liberated because

Mayur had pushed her away whenever she initiated or sought intimacy. Neerja kept flowing like a river carrying her pain and hurt within her.

She did not realise that she was compromising her health in the process. Her hormonal imbalance struck and that led to a lot of hair loss. It was tough for her to deal with the situation and pick up the loose strands of hair from the drain and flooring after a bath, or her pillow every morning. She decided to go to the city for treatment which was forty kilometres away and only Diya came along. The doctor told her that the hair fall was due to high levels of stress. The salty water in the place where Mayur was working was also damaging. Diya who had lovely black hair as a child also had rough brown hair now, they both were on a downward spiral.

Neerja felt that these compromises had to be made to keep the family together. One must go through challenges together to strengthen the relationship. Hardships test your commitment. However, it was only Neerja who seemed to be working towards maintaining a relationship and any effort from Mayur was absolutely missing! One evening, at a party, Mayur consumed excessive alcohol and Neerja drove them home to safeguard the respect of the family. But, none of her efforts seemed to move Mayur. Her daughter was closely observing the dynamics in the relationship. Children are good judges of character.

The Universe heard Diya's prayers and with the help of Neerja's father, Mayur was transferred back close to Neerja's parents' home. Neerja's parents who had been supporting Neerja financially throughout her marriage supplied them with every household item. Her husband did not allow her to run the house. They did not even have a joint account in the ten years they were together. No one imagined that Mayur was growing more bitter. One night after they returned home from dinner at Neerja's parents' house, Mayur who was in one of his nasty moods, entered the house quickly and locked the door from inside before Neerja or Diya could step in. Neerja and Diya kept ringing the bell. He opened the door only after they had been screaming for a while. This infuriated Neerja and they entered into a severe argument, which made Mayur turn violent as usual. This time Neerja picked herself off the floor and walked out with her daughter.

That night, Neerja along with her dad went to the police station to file a complaint about domestic violence. Neerja was visiting a police station for the first time. The inspector asked her to submit an application and Neerja quickly handed it over to the constable. He looked at the letter written in cursive with immaculate English and let out a hearty laugh. She needed to write in Hindi; Neerja was good at Hindi and she drafted another letter. She was shocked when they read the subject of the letter and remarked, *"It is the duty of a husband to manage his wife even if that requires force, these girls learn the English alphabet and come here to sob just because they get slapped by their husbands sometimes."*

Neerja started receiving phone calls from constables to take back her complaint. Some of these were women who were bribed by Mayur. Neerja realised that corruption was prevalent even in the system that is meant to safeguard women. The questions by the lawyers created unrest in her. The court seemed like a very cold place where everything moved at a snail's pace. Neerja remembered what she had read long ago, *"Justice delayed is justice denied."* The court proceedings were like prolonged meetings. It is a haven for liars as they are unashamed and benefit from the delay in judgement but it tires those who have to repeat their truth a hundred times until it is heard; it may or may not be believed. As a character streak, Neerja betrayed herself and her dad and took the case back. Mayur and she were advised to spend a few months together before they came to any conclusion. This worked to her husband's advantage and he knew that not even Neerja's parents could free her from this bondage. She would be his slave for life! Neerja was a prisoner who was scared to step into the light.

Neerja spent her days staring outside the window of the living room like a caged bird. She had closed all doors and no help could reach her. *She only realised later in life that help was always close, she had to simply turn inwards.* A reservoir of guidance was available. She just needed to tap that source. One day *Brahma Kumari* Sister Shivani came as a guest speaker to the school where Neerja worked as a teacher. When Neerja heard her speak, she felt that she was watching someone from another planet. *For the first time, she was in the company of an awakened being.* Her parents were religious but she did not know that a person can be spiritual.

Neerja started listening to Sister Shivani on television. *It felt like meeting a long-lost friend.* On Sundays she would watch *Satyamev Jayate* hosted by Aamir Khan; Neerja wept watching some of the women share stories similar to hers. These women had walked out of those toxic relationships on their own. Around this same time, Neerja discovered *A New Earth* by Eckhart Tolle, *every word in that book resonated with her. Listening to her inner voice led to Neerja's spiritual awakening. This was the first turning point in Neerja's life.*

She had reached a fork in the road. She gathered her courage and left Mayur forever. The victory of good over evil is inevitable. Diya was also all set with her little suitcase. Neerja and Diya were now going to begin their new life independently. Neerja was out in the world leaving behind familiarity, the only thing those years of abuse had offered to her. To her surprise, this felt liberating. When you shed the burden of a façade you know the pleasure of authenticity. They say when you are on the path, encounters with like-minded people can be expected. Books fall from shelves. Signs are everywhere. You find your tribe.

Diya was nourished with joy; she blossomed like a flower. She met the person her mom truly was, for the first time. Neerja laughed, joked, danced and was the most popular person in the organization. They had to take care of everything themselves but this was a small price to pay for their freedom; Mayur turning the doorknob upon his return from the office used to give Diya goosebumps in their old home.

Victims of abuse often release their pent-up anger on others. Neerja too struggled for years with anger issues. She would lose her temper with Diya when she was stressed and then regret it for hours. During this phase of her life, Neerja got a chance to attend mindfulness training by monks from Plum village who were disciples of Thich Nhat Hanh and was named the *stable equanimity of the heart* by them. Her friend taught her affirmations and gifted her *You Can Heal Your Life* by Louise Hay. Neerja wore beads and meditated every morning.

In spite of everything, Neerja had failed to leave behind her strongest pattern. The emptiness in her life had to be filled. Most men liked her for her vivaciousness and energy, but she mistook their liking for love. Her daughter and friends soon identified this pattern in Neerja. Neerja would get rebellious if she was asked to be watchful. Even men who cared for her could not help her to differentiate between friendship and a relationship. There seemed to be a constant inner conflict in her between the good angel and the bad angel.

A WOUNDED SOUL

Neerja valued human connections above everything. Her classroom was a life class where every individual was encouraged to find their voice. Her students shared their joys and challenges with her and described her as a breath of fresh air. Neerja was inspired by her *gurus* growing up and now she was living those ideals. She would get opportunities to accompany her students for competitions to other schools and on trips. During these expeditions, she would appreciate the culture of each institution and learn their educational philosophy. Neerja made several trips to Goa with Diya and a solo trip to Manali and was referred to as the teacher with the tattoos. She practised her tea meditation and had a morning ritual that prepared her for the day ahead.

People around her began to notice the light that Neerja was blessed with. Her life had a purpose far greater than herself. Her character flaw had been blocking that light like clouds hiding the sun. She found her way to the library once again and the Universe lined up all its messengers for her. Wayne Dyer, Eckhart Tolle, Rumi, Swami Vivekananda, J Krishnamurti, Osho, Gary Zukav, Adhyashanti, Sadhguru, Marriane Williamson… infinite voices spoke to her. Neerja would spend her weekends searching for these gems in bookstores. She watched *Eat, Pray, Love* and played the part of Julia Roberts at one of the school events. She cared for those who led as well as those who served; Neerja *recognised the Buddha in everyone.* People warmed up to her instantly because of her smile.

Diya followed her around like a lamb. They had struggled together but had now created this beautiful world for themselves. Neerja was reassured that God loves everyone. They lived in a small studio apartment with limited resources, but their home was filled with joy. Neerja would still return to her blind spot occasionally. She would make a man the hero of her life, this would always blur the boundary between fiction and reality for her. She would put men on a pedestal and would go to any extent to please them. She would ignore her practice, her work and Diya. She would fixate like an addict. On the other end, Neerja was quick to point out the flaws in a system and nothing would stop her from speaking the truth. Her opinions were respected at work and she was a threat to anyone who misused their power.

Her coffee breaks with her friends led to more spiritual discoveries. They would talk endlessly about their spiritual journeys. When one of her friends became a victim of office politics, Neerja stood up for her. The owner of the school valued the truth in Neerja's words. Neerja was a loyal friend and never left the side of a friend in need. Neerja kept challenging herself and studied day and night to prepare for interviews in other places. She had a vision board and did her affirmations with faith. They got their chance and within a few years boarded the flight to join a new school in a big city. Neerja was always a nomadic soul.

Neerja made a huge leap in her career, which came with its own set of challenges. She had to learn a new curriculum and had to get comfortable with using technology in classrooms. Diya and Neerja explored the city during weekends. They were impressed with the choices a big city offers. Shopping became their favourite activity and they bonded over it. They made new friends and memories. Neerja was handed additional responsibilities at work and was often praised for her efforts. However, there was no remuneration for the added work. They were always given a small studio apartment with the justification that they were a small family. She was even paid less than her counterparts despite her work profile in the organisation! It was taken for granted that she would be obligated for her daughter's free education and their housing, though these perks came with her job and this was not an exception made in her case.

Neerja and Diya had assumed that they would be free from oppression after leaving Mayur. Yet, Neerja was now dealing with the unfairness in the system. Single women are expected to work harder or equivalent to others without any consideration. They manage their home and work but are rarely commended for it. They are viewed either as needy or tough women who should put up with anything for a lack of choice. Sometimes people throw extra work at them assuming that they have no familial commitments just because they do not have a husband. Neerja observed that very few single women occupied top positions in organisations. Equality for women at home and work is still a distant dream in many parts of the world. Her friendship with Om, a gay colleague, became a scoop for gossip mongers. Diya stood by her mom and encouraged her mom to have a life beyond work.

During a short break, Neerja planned a trip to Puducherry. Travelling had always been one of her soul therapies. *This trip gave Neerja a fresh vision for her life.* She visited the

Aurobindo Ashram and learnt about the life of Sri Aurobindo and Mother. This surreal experience had a deep impact on Neerja. Neerja affirmed that she would establish a spiritual retreat for people who were starved of connection in their stressful, modern lives. *Her life was a message and she was going to put it to use.* Neerja visited Auroville on her way back and was inspired by their educational philosophy. She carried a few books and a picture of Sri Aurobindo and Mother with her, Diya placed it on their altar with their idol of *Sai Baba*. This sacred corner anchored Neerja. *She wanted to give others a way of life, a path to walk on. She was still unaware where this path would lead her or those who followed.*

Chapter 14

Neerja wanted to bring about a radical change in the existing working system, but every time she raised her voice against something, it was silenced by people who disliked the truth. These people fiercely defended the lies they had fed themselves and others, which had made them comfortable. The truth is unsettling. Most people act as advocates for change but fear it the most, they remain stuck in their repetitive thinking patterns and never see the light.

Neerja changed several organisations but could not get rid of her old baggage. Soon mother and daughter joined the rat race. They had no time for themselves due to their rigorous schedule and increasing demands at work. Diya lost her health and was mostly confined to her room. They had no friends, no time for interactions. Like everyone else around them, Neerja and Diya had also been reduced to robots. The apathy in human interactions tipped the balance. Desperation called for help and Neerja reached out for her drug, she got in touch with a young man who had shown interest in her and asked him to take her on a long drive. She wanted to escape this drudgery and gave herself permission to indulge. As most Indian women she had put the demands of motherhood before herself. Her body was meant to bring life into this world… her personal needs did not exist.

At work, Neerja encountered several kinds of women. There were the compulsive workaholics whose partners were also workaholics; the privileged ones who did not need the job but did not wish to resign as homemakers; the dynamic ones who seemed to have it all under control; the single women who seemed to have married the organisation; the dominant ones who passed on the work to others and always walked away with the credit, and the shirkers, who survived the longest. Neerja did not fit into any of these moulds. It was disparaging to work with people who lived in their elitist cocoons, but now Neerja knew her worth as a professional. She was not someone to be messed with. Her friends admired how she maintained a perfect work-life balance.

Yet, in the privacy of her own space, Neerja was getting overwhelmed. She was tired of putting up a strong exterior... the struggles of a single woman were taking their toll on her. Something broke on the inside and she was carried away by the strong currents... she was unanchored. Neerja decided to fulfil her desires as a woman. She would give herself to men hoping that they would fall in love with her and promise her the security that she now sought precariously. She kept lying to Diya and deceiving herself. And then, one fine morning, looking at herself in the mirror, Neerja felt terrible! She could see the truth staring back at her. Those younger men were entertaining Neerja because they would not have to bother about a commitment with a middle-aged single woman, they did not really care for her. Addictions are perils of the unconscious living in big cities. People develop compulsive disorders like overworking, binging, shopping and speed dating. Cities house many lonely lives. The city-bred live in constant fear of getting redundant; they have a compulsive need to stay updated or to upgrade themselves.

Neerja befriended a middle-aged Italian artist, Ross. She wanted to experience everything that her marriage had failed to offer. Most of her time was spent with Ross who was recently divorced and emotionally needy. Constant texts and phone calls from him took her attention away from everything else in her life. She was consumed by it. Diya warned Neerja several times that she was getting misled but this would lead to fights between them. Their relationship reached its breaking point and Diya packed her bags one day to leave for her grandparents' home. At this point, Neerja begged Diya for another chance.

By this time though, Neerja had gotten deeply involved. Ross would be unwilling to leave her alone and would always cling to her. He slowly started to poison Neerja against Diya. Neerja was completely under his grip. She would not go home on vacations but travel with him. She always wanted to belong to a man and Ross was fuelling her fantasy. They had their first argument over another woman who was twenty years younger than him, whom he started to desire physically. Neerja expressed her displeasure and it was met with an utterly shocking reaction. He dragged her out of his home and broke up with her. His children whom she cooked and cared for also turned their backs on her. Neerja, true to her nature, could not reason out and blamed herself for offending him! She begged Ross to give their relationship another chance. The earlier pattern resurfaced and once again Neerja's life turned into a cycle of abuse.

There is still a lack of awareness around mental health issues in several parts of India. There need to be more forums and talks around these topics which require early diagnosis and intervention so that so many lives are not lost in the darkness. Neerja was suffering from Stockholm syndrome and she needed a hand to guide her out. One day suddenly, Neerja woke up feeling emptier. She confided in Diya who told her that Neerja needed to act fast to preserve herself. Neerja put herself in self-isolation during the holidays and cut off from Ross. Her soul was wounded. She wanted answers so that she could quit blaming herself. Glennon Doyle's *Love Warrior* arrived in time. Neerja knew that she had to sit with this *"hot loneliness"* and *"not let this pain get wasted"*. Neerja discovered that Ross had a sex addiction and was a covert narcissist. He was in therapy now.

Neerja started showing withdrawal symptoms, she convinced Diya to allow her to try online dating just as a distraction. She had no idea about the rules of online dating, she just jumped into the game. The likes from a large number of men gave her an instant high and she started to open up to anyone who was listening. She started to date Jude whom she met online, she would share pictures of herself and her activities with him and he would also reciprocate, she was settling into this online arrangement when Jude made a sudden plan to visit her by sea, Neerja was exhilarated and eagerly waited to meet him in person.

A week later she received an urgent mail from him asking for help. He wrote that his ship had been attacked by pirates and he had lost his passport in the sea. He needed money to get new documents to cross the border and would have to ship a consignment to her. Neerja prayed to *Sai Baba* for Jude's safety; *surprisingly her inner voice told her a different story: He had fabricated this tale and just wanted money.* Neerja refused to send the money and asked him to return, this plan made Jude give himself away. Neerja blocked him and consulted a friend for advice. Neerja was dumbfounded by what she found out.

She had narrowly escaped an online dating scam. Jude's identity was unreal. Neerja realised that she could not only have lost a lot of money but her dignity as well. He had some of her personal information, as well as some extremely private pictures that were inappropriate for the public platform that he could misuse; this would have endangered Diya's life as well. Her pattern had grown into a disease that was infecting their already tough life. They had their own struggles; Diya would compare her circumstances with the other kids in her school. While they would be waiting for a cab outside a supermarket, they would watch other families leave in their cars. They would have to carry their bags of groceries up the stairs to their apartment, help was never offered by neighbours or those around. Once Neerja fell ill and Diya ran around in the hospital arranging appointments, paying bills and collecting medicines. Mayur would only call Diya twice or thrice a year. He never asked her if she needed any help. Neerja had not filed for a divorce because she no longer trusted the broken system.

She was tired of her interactions with promiscuous, polyamorous, patronising and predatorial men online; all reeking of male chauvinism. She found out that a separate set of rules existed for men and women even in online dating. Women must dress in a certain way, be home before it gets dark in the real world and even tread cautiously in the virtual world out of fear of being defamed. They crawl through a minefield all their lives. A lot of these men were either married or held respectable positions in society; they just lacked spice in their lives. Neerja never understood the concept of open relationships. You either stay committed or quit. These men were making an unhealthy use of these platforms. Their family, reputation, work, time and convenience mattered; women were expected to oblige. *Neerja was aware that the world has all kinds of people and she wondered why she was only attracting painful experiences into her life. Once more she had reached a fork in the road and she took the road less travelled.*

PART TWO

SANGAM - UNITY OF MIND, BODY AND SOUL

Chapter 15

One fine day in your life, if you find yourself asking questions like, *why am I suffering? Is suffering avoidable? Is there an end to my suffering?* it means you are at the crossroads. The Universe is offering you a chance to redesign your life. Neerja had already trodden the path of blame and was tired of playing the victim. She looked around for help, for some guidance, but there was none. She sat down at this juncture and closed her eyes. She travelled back to the spiritual dots in her life. *The dots signified the phases of her growth. Neerja finally began to connect the dots.*

Her life seemed like a game of snakes and ladders; she had made a lot of mistakes but had progressed as well. She no longer wanted her life to depend on the rolling of a dice or chance. The question was, could she change that? Could she alter the rules of the game? She went back to the beginning of her life. We cannot choose our parents or the families we are born into. Some of us are lucky and have a good start while others have a rough one. What then, could she change or fix in her childhood that had led her to develop a complex mind? She had already lost her brother and could not amend that relationship. Her ego had prevented her from being with Varun before he left for his heavenly abode. Now, she could only preserve the pleasantness of his presence on Earth.

She moved towards the next pain body within her. Neerja

was closer to her parents now and shared everything with them, but she was still angry. She was resentful because they had failed as parents at two crucial moments which changed the direction of Varun's and Neerja's lives. They had hesitated to pull Varun and Neerja out of their misery; a consequence of their blind choices. Neerja had decided to keep this resentment covered as she was scared to lose her parents. Her disappointment with her parents would sometimes find an escape in the heat of an argument with them or when she would talk about Varun's and her pain of abandonment to Diya. She had learnt to cope with that reality by not confronting it, but the wound had not healed. Was there a remedy? Was there a permanent cure?

Neerja reflected on her parents' decisions. They had simply passed on their dreams to their children. Having a government job and marrying a well-settled person were the best options according to her parents and so they believed that they had taken the right decisions for Varun and Neerja. It was their conditioning that did not allow them to look at the reality of things. Neerja was still unable to reconcile, she felt that once they knew that Varun and Neerja were not happy on those paths, they should have supported them to switch to other paths.

Choosing an unfamiliar or unconventional path does not symbolise failure; unfortunately for a lot of families in India, it still does. The older generations had to struggle to pursue their dreams due to the lack of funds and resources in large families but most Indian fathers refuse to make timely investments in their children's dreams and lives even today, they do not realise that they will reap the rewards along with their children in the long run. The children will be happy because of the opportunities they provided them with for their growth rather than holding back. There is no fixed marriageable age for a girl; girls must have the liberty to marry when they are ready or not marry if it does not feel right. It is not a woman's duty alone to make a marriage work; if marriages depend on equal partnership, then why is the entire burden put on a woman's shoulder?

Would holding on to these grudges set Neerja free? What could she do? If you lost the first innings in a match, would you stop playing or plan on doing worse? You would, instead, come up with a fool-proof strategy and turn the odds in your favour in the second innings. Neerja decided that she was going to use her past as a springboard and not get shackled by it. *The spiritual dots in her life were like tiny revelations and she started to reflect on each one.* Neerja's quest was ongoing. She chose to focus on the good things that her parents had done for Varun and her rather than holding them accountable for all her problems just because they had decided to get her married. You should not pass a verdict without listening to both sides. Her mind had declared them guilty and absolved her.

How were Varun and Neerja responsible for their parents' decisions? Towards the end of his school life, Varun was getting restless with the academic pressure which was not allowing him to follow his interest in cricket and other outdoor activities. He also showed an inclination towards the balanced life a government job promises. Neerja on the other hand had gone astray and was not interested in getting her master's degree. Marriage to Mayur seemed like a quick solution. She realised that they were not resolute enough to oppose the plans their parents made for them. Neerja now had to come to terms with the truth.

She began to dig deeper into her mind for a better understanding. Her dad was always occupied with his extended family and this led to the fights between him and their mother. Neerja had also felt neglected as a child and hated the attention that he showered on her cousins. Most of these relatives disappear during bad times and resurface when they see you flourish. But, Neerja knew that not everyone was bad, their family friends and a few relatives were truly fond of her parents. After her marriage to Mayur, Neerja had made several attempts to be a part of his family but he always kept her away; Diya had grown up only with her mother, and this had deprived her of the joy of belonging to a big family. Undoubtedly, every large family has fights, but the happiness gets multiplied as well. Festivals and special occasions are a grand affair; the joint family system makes India unique. Her parents grew up with these values and they would never change. *Neerja's resistance would only hurt her.*

Neerja now reflected on her delusions. She knew that she would set high goals for herself but did not work towards achieving them. The fear of disappointment had made her take rash steps in her childhood and this had caused her parents a lot of pain and humiliation. Things could have turned unfavourable but she always came out unscathed. She stopped to wonder; she had heard her *inner voice* in those moments and was always protected. *She was becoming more aware of the love that always existed in her life.*

Neerja was one of those few privileged women in India who had been provided with the best education by her parents and was allowed to pursue a subject that she loved from an expensive college. Her dad was always her greatest cheerleader; he was the man behind her professional success. He went for every interview that she took and stayed up for nights to help her complete her education. Though Neerja had to struggle to achieve success at work, she had many great women mentors who believed in her capabilities. She was offered leadership roles in some organisations and new opportunities for learning and growth. She admired women who broke the mould. She had won the respect of her colleagues for her ability to multitask and had a well-paying job that allowed her to provide Diya with the best learning opportunities and exposure. *Varun did not get another chance, Neerja was humbled by this realisation.*

Chapter 16

When she began to sift the evidence, she learnt that we all have an **inner voice** trying to guide us and show us the way, yet we let the demons inside our heads take control. We get caught up in the narrative that the mind weaves and the truth is veiled; longing to be unearthed. She remembered how she felt alive when she was connected with people or was teaching; those moments were like signposts strewn in her path; they were directing her towards her calling. *Neerja awakened to the reality that life is not a series of random events, it has a purpose.*

Neerja shuddered for a while as she continued to reminisce about her early life, she remembered how after an epiphany she would hit another rock bottom, she could never achieve stability. She scratched beneath the surface of her deepest wound. Why did she need a saviour? She had grappled with this pattern for the longest time, and it was time for her to gear up to find her answers, she racked her brains to find out what caused this need. Neerja had a flash; her path was destined right from her birth; every time she drifted from her path, she felt empty and she clung to someone else for meaning and purpose. She realised that *the epiphanies happened on the path and she hit rock bottoms whenever she strayed.*

More questions arose in her mind. Were men using her neediness to abuse her? Why was she inviting the same type of men into her life? Neerja believed in true love but had always attracted unhealthy relationships. She went back to the drawing board and looked at each one of them. She was infatuated with Tejas because of his intelligence and their common interests, he on the other hand had clearly told her what he wanted out of the friendship; Neerja had fed her illusion. Her *intention* to marry Mayur was wrong, he offered an escape. All the other men only existed to fill the void in her life. Could she blame them entirely?

How they had treated Neerja could not be justified but she had to forgive them to get to the root of the problem. She recognized that they too had problems that they had not confronted and dealt with. The fear of failing in the eyes of others and the monotony and drudgery of her lonely life had placed her at the mercy of these men.

Neerja sat down to meditate. She was always living in the future. She would feel bored and restless like *Holden Caulfield* in *The Catcher in the Rye* in her early life. She was never at peace with herself or the present moment. She kept changing places, partners and plans to feel good and yet, she felt empty. *There was a constant mismatch between her expectations and reality.* She always felt people were causing her pain, places were unsuitable, life was not fair and so she had to run and run away from all that is. She wondered if she was honouring the life that had been bestowed on her; whether she was counting her blessings.

India teaches you reverence; there are people here who struggle to get two meals a day and still have faith. Were her complaints relevant? She started focusing on her blessings and she lost count. She woke up feeling grateful for another day. Being present is the greatest gift you can give to yourself and to your loved ones. She started taking responsibility for her life by cherishing small moments with Diya, her conversations with friends and her nature walks. Everything suddenly seemed meaningful; there is greatness in simplicity, ordinariness and in the present moment.

Neerja had shared several beautiful moments with Varun, her parents, Mayur, her friends, the men in her life, colleagues, her students and Diya; she thanked the Universe for each one of them.

Nothing is wasted in life. Your time in *The Earth School* is precious; this whole journey is about transforming or reinventing yourself. There are no chance encounters, every experience you have here is either a blessing or a lesson; when you begin to see hurtful people, harmful patterns, toxic environments or excruciating pain as possibilities for a change you begin to welcome each one of them. Acceptance should be our driving force, when you reject something, you lose an opportunity for growth.

Neerja pondered about the violence that Mayur had inflicted on her. What about the injustice that she faced as a woman? How could she justify the lack of consideration that others had shown to her? Neerja knew that most girls are conditioned to believe that they should be subservient to men; they watch their fathers ill-treat their mothers and how gender stereotypes function in society. Could all this have happened to Neerja without her consent? Of course, a man can overpower a woman physically but how can women empower themselves? Neerja did not want to acquit men from their misdoings; she wanted to protect herself and other women like her. *She was determined to find solutions; she was tired of focusing on the problems in her life.*

Neerja became aware that her self-worth had depended on a

man's validation. It was time for her to get rid of this belief. A woman should be invested in her own growth not beg a man for his time, attention or support. It is human to love another person but you should value yourself above all. Self-love is not equivalent to being selfish, it is being aware of your boundaries and not allowing anyone to treat you with disrespect. Love can be cultivated; you do not have to seek it, and those who truly love you will never ill treat you. Our expectations may not always be met by people, organizations or systems, but we can treat ourselves better and teach them how to treat us; we can show them the way.

Neerja could have exercised the *power of choice* in most of those situations. She could have walked away. By choosing to stay she had allowed those men to take her for granted. *"You should never be at a table where respect is no longer being served."* Sometimes we do not get the support from our families and the society that we hoped for, Neerja had experienced this first-hand and so she decided that she would turn her dream of building a spiritual centre into reality. She may not be able to save every wounded soul but she would give shelter to some until they learn to depend on their own inner strength. *She had drawn inspiration from the spiritual masters on her journey; every book, talk show, interview that had guided her, was a spiritual dot.* Help always appeared when she sought it.

Neerja's mind was fresh and she made a headway on the path she had chosen. She was curious to find out when she would hit the next *milestone.*

Chapter 17

Neerja found out that her progress was hindered because she was detached from her body. Her health had deteriorated over the years and she weighed a hundred and eighty pounds. She did lose weight multiple times and got into shape only to win the approval of Mayur or other men. When they would not treat her any better, she would go back to the same eating habits and would stop exercising. Stress was her worst enemy; she would binge eat every time she was overwhelmed with work and additional duties. She would try to cover up for her odd body weight by buying clothes, makeup and accessories but she was not confident like before. She was in denial and refused to do anything about it.

She took care of her appearance only when she was at work or heading out for a date. During one of the vacations from school, she was unable to speak. Her throat hurt and she coughed all night. Neerja was terrified, she had quit smoking and drinking but thought that she was experiencing some side effects and had a major illness. She coughed blood one day and had to rush to the doctor. Diya was the only one by her side while the tests were being conducted. At that moment Neerja understood that she had a responsibility towards herself and Diya which was far greater than her addictions. She shivered at the thought of being hospitalised with no one to take care of Diya and the huge medical expenses that they could not afford.

She prayed for help. As it turned out, her diagnosis was not complex and she was told, with few lifestyle changes and medicines, she could be on her road to recovery soon. Neerja got back from the hospital grateful for another chance and with a new resolve. She made time for herself and restarted her morning ritual. She never missed her walks and started reconnecting with her body. She had more stamina and would always be fresh to start her day. *Her mind and body finally reunited and existed in harmony; she stopped punishing her body when her mind was upset.* She would meditate and clear her mind during her *me-time* every morning. Everyone around her began to notice the positive changes that Neerja was making in her life.

Mayur had ill-treated her for years by body-shaming her. Neerja was on her journey of self-love and she was accepting of the beauty of her body. The ideals of beauty and body shape that the world constantly feeds us with, must be ignored. We were created perfectly in the image of God. No one has the right to belittle us because our worth is not determined by the colour of our eyes, hair or skin, or by whether we fit into a large, medium or small frame but by the imprints, we leave on *The Earth School* by our goodness, kindness and usefulness. This awareness changes the way we look at ourselves and others.

Neerja had also experienced the emptiness and quick death of relationships that were only based on physical needs. The union of two bodies without the union of their minds always ends in shame, hurt and betrayal. Diya had suffered due to her weak immunity as a child and Neerja started focusing on a nutritious diet, healthy habits and a balanced life for both of them. Children spend all their time in front of gadgets, they do various activities to sharpen the mind but the body must not be ignored. There is no greater joy than being amidst nature, artificial stimulations can never replace the magic of the Universe. *Neerja kept moving steadily on her path.*

Chapter 18

Have you ever stared at the ocean in awe of its vastness or wondered about your insignificance gazing at the night sky? Have you felt like a tiny speck in the Universe or questioned whether you even matter in the larger scheme of things? Have you ever speculated about the meaning of your life and your existence? These are pertinent questions and their answers are available. You just have to travel beyond your sense perception...

Neerja was entering the spiritual realm now; she had travelled further on the path. She believed that Varun's soul had chosen Diya's body to fulfil its purpose in *The Earth School*. Our spirit gives meaning to our whole life, our mind and body are tools meant to serve our soul's purpose here in this school.

Neerja looked around; she noticed that human beings were struggling to preserve their sanity. We are stuck in traffic, our flight is delayed, the cashier at the grocery store makes an error while billing our items or our children disturb us in the middle of our online meeting, these are just some scenarios that most of us face in our daily lives and if we manage to come out of these without losing our cool, we feel victorious. We view this as self-mastery. Neerja sat down to write her reflections in her journal, something she was used to doing since she was young. Why do we spend most of our lives in our minds? Humans are much invested in the growth of their minds and body; we have overtaken other species on Earth and are trying to invade other planets. We constantly challenge our physical boundaries but very few of us are invested in our inner growth. The power that we are building is only external. *This imbalance between our inner growth and outer growth is the prime cause of our misery.* We are obsessed with dominance over other life forms but are slaves of our own monkey minds and the machines with artificial intelligence created by us. Our estimation of growth is limited; it is confined to the man-made world. However, there is no limit to our growth in the spiritual realm; we experience expansion and grasp that our being is infinite like the ocean's; there is no separation between us and the Universe, there is oneness. The *spiritual dots in Neerja's life were her moments of oneness,* she kept following the signs.

Neerja was now nearing another *milestone* on her journey. She sat down to meditate in silence. *She was at a junction where our mind, body and soul unite; we reach this point through self-discovery.* Neerja was the presence – the observer of her thoughts. The presence resides in the now in a blissful state of true joy, love and peace.

Chapter 19

Neerja was amazed, the path that she had chosen to walk on had taken her inwards. She knew the destination was close, she had to sit in silence. She reflected on her previous thought; we are so focused on preserving our sanity that we have forgotten about the *sanctity* of human life and human interactions. How we treat ourselves and others, defines the quality of the connections we make in *The Earth School*. Do we question our prejudices, beliefs, judgements, opinions and perceptions about people? Do we get past our anger, resentment, hatred, suspicion and jealousy and embrace the holiness in every being?

The Buddhist monks had taught Neerja to honour the Buddha in everyone; she had to now learn to honour that power of life within her. The point where our mind, body and soul unite, leads us to our inner sanctuary that seats our *Sanctum Sanctorum*. God or our life force resides here. Our *inner voice* summons us from here.

Neerja figured out that we should never allow anyone to violate that sacred space. She decided to put out a "no entry sign" here so that no one at work, home or even in an intimate relationship would have access to it. She had to set clear boundaries and *preserve the sanctity of her life force*. All of us have an energy field, we can misuse its influence to hurt others and harm the planet or use it to benefit others and contribute to *The Earth School*. Neerja always wanted to find love; she never realised that you do not need to find something that already exists within you! You are pure love, joy and peace. All of us are sent to this Earth with a treasure chest, we just need to awaken to its presence within us. We need to keep it safeguarded.

Neerja visits her sanctum sanctorum often now and invites every wandering soul she meets on her odyssey to discover that sacred space within themselves.

POWER OF KNOWING

Neerja reflected on what separated her past from her present. Her ignorance was the cause of her suffering in the past. She lacked the knowledge that she now possessed; *she was now endowed with the power of knowing.* We treat ourselves and others recklessly until we are awakened to the presence of God or the life force in each one of us. Conscious beings live responsibly and show respect towards all forms of life. The power of knowing fills the present moment with meaning, it reminds you of the sanctity of your presence in *The Earth School* and of the sanctity of your actions and interactions in the now. It changes the way we think, act or behave with others.

The power of knowing breaks several myths about spirituality. Spirituality does not necessitate renunciation or penance, it is not a luxury of the rich, a panacea for human suffering or a subject to be disregarded by the sceptics; it does not belong to any race, gender or class. It is the truth, a *deep knowing that there is no separation between the life force and us. The power of life resides in us.* Spirituality is not something that is defined by how we dress, what we eat or where we live; the truth does not require any external replication. It is the basis of every human life.

With the help of this new knowledge, even during a crisis, we do not wait for any external help or rush to our meditation pillow to centre ourselves, we know that everything that happens, happens for the greater good of all; we may not see the light for a while but the sun never stops shining. Spirituality is about self-help and don't we all need it? It empowers us to choose love over fear. The spiritual masters had the power of knowing so they turned inwards to look for answers. Neerja was living unconsciously in her past; people and work were just a means to an end but now she had a deeper understanding of her connections and commitments in *The Earth School.*

We do our best with what we know at any given moment… *Neerja now consciously exercised her power of knowing at every step of her odyssey, and this was her spiritual practice.* Neerja knew that the message she had received must not be lost; its efficacy would increase with its transference. The presence of seeds in a fruit is nature's way of teaching us, that knowledge has to be passed on.

Neerja vowed to spread her message to the whole world and to share her practice with others. *Her legacy would be a new world – a world of knowers.*

GLOSSARY

Dhaba – A roadside food stall

Devis – Goddesses

Dupatta – A length of material worn by women from South Asia, arranged in two folds over the chest and thrown back around the shoulders, typically with a salwar kameez.

Ghee – Clarified butter

Guru – A teacher

Hanuman – A Hindu god and divine *vanara* (monkey) who is blessed with immortality and special strength and power.

Hanuman Chalisa – Hanuman Chalisa is a timeless ode to devotion. Lord Hanuman is known for his devotion to Lord Ram and is considered to be the embodiment of faith, surrender, and devotion.

Laddoos – An Indian sweet made from a mixture of flour, sugar, and shortening, which is shaped into a ball.

Lord Shiva – Shiva (Siva) is one of the most important gods in the Hindu pantheon and is considered a member of the holy trinity *(trimurti)* of Hinduism with Brahma and Vishnu.

Mangalsutra – The word *mangal* means auspicious and *sutra* means thread – together mangalsutra means an auspicious thread uniting the souls. The groom ties the auspicious thread around the bride's neck on the day of their holy nuptial signifying that their relationship would be as auspicious as the thread.

Navratris – An annual Hindu festival celebrated over nine days in September – October. Observed throughout India, it commemorates the slaying of demons by Rama and the goddess Durga; in some places, it is dedicated to all female deities.

Pheras – The seven Pheras or the Saptapadi is the true essence of a Vedic wedding. Only when the bride and the groom take the seven vows keeping the holy pyre as the witness, they are referred to as married. The bride and the groom hold their hands and take seven rounds around the Agni and promise to be with each other for eternity.

Roka – It is an official announcement of your relationship in front of the world. It signifies that the bride and groom have accepted each other. Along with this, this is the first function when families officially meet each other.

Sai Baba – Sai Baba of Shirdi was an Indian spiritual master who is regarded by his devotees to be a manifestation of Sri Dattaguru and identified as a saint and a fakir. He was revered by both his Hindu and Muslim devotees during, as well as after his lifetime.

Tandava – Tandava (also spelt as *Tāṇḍavam*) also known as *Tāṇḍava Natyam*, is a divine dance performed by Hindu god Shiva.

Vaishno Devi – An important Hindu temple dedicated to Vaishno Devi located in Katra at the Trikuta Mountains within the Indian Union territory of Jammu and Kashmir.